YOUR KNOWLEDGE HAS VALUE

Bibliographic information published by the German National Library:

The German National Library lists this publication in the National Bibliography;
detailed bibliographic data are available on the Internet at http://dnb.dnb.de .

Imprint:

Copyright © 2019 GRIN Verlag
Print and binding: Books on Demand GmbH, Norderstedt Germany
ISBN: 9783346057976

This book at GRIN:

https://www.grin.com/document/503323

Fanny S. Alam

Transwomen Gap for a Formal Work Attainment in Indonesia. A Part of the Sustainable Development Goals

GRIN Verlag

GRIN - Your knowledge has value

Since its foundation in 1998, GRIN has specialized in publishing academic texts by students, college teachers and other academics as e-book and printed book. The website www.grin.com is an ideal platform for presenting term papers, final papers, scientific essays, dissertations and specialist books.

Visit us on the internet:

http://www.grin.com/

http://www.facebook.com/grincom

http://www.twitter.com/grin_com

Transwomen Gap for a Formal Work Attainment as a Part of

Indonesia's SDGS Implementation Constrains

Fanny S. Alam
Coordinator of Bandung's School of Peace Indonesia

Abstract

The Indonesian Government's commitment to signing Sustainable Development Goals (SDGs) from 2015- 2030 views their significant development platform in a purpose to create sustainable developing aspects for more prosperous societies and the country. It is translated into Presidential Act no. 59/2017 about The Implementation of Achievement towards Sustainable Development Goals with an emphasis of three principles, such as Acceleration, Funding, and Inclusion.

Inclusion in SDGs means leaving no one behind, ensuring that all the targets must meet the interests of all people of nations without any exceptions as stated by UNSTATS, and it covers vulnerable or marginalized groups, including LGBTI. 12 UN entities endorse the statement underlining the importance of LGBTI's participation for countries' development process.

In contradict, the LGBTI in Indonesia have faced serious challenges, principally about their human rights. Transwomen are considered repressed for their right to be properly employed. A formal work attainment for the group tends to create another negative concern due to the employers' highlight to their sexuality not to their capacity. The paper elaborates how their gap occurs based on the methods of direct observation toward keypersons as well as literature and media study. It comes with an expectation that in long terms, the group might be employed for formal works as maintained for informal ones currently.

Keywords: SDGs, Inclusion, Transwomen, Work, LGBTI

Contents

1. INTRODUCTION

Every Indonesian citizen is born with basic rights later on translated into human rights. The implementation of human rights actually has been acknowledged in the Indonesian Constitution 1945 which credentials the citizens' rights to empower themselves economically, politically, socially, and culturally. As mentioned in Act 27 verse 1 about the citizens' right to be treated equally in politics and government system and their duty to enforce law and existing government. Act 28 mentions the citizens' rights to express themselves through verbal and written statements, to gather in a union or organization as long as they obey the principles of Pancasila (five basics of the state's principle) and have a moral responsibility addressing the process and its conveyance publicly. In terms of social and culture, Act 31 verse 1 emphasizes the citizens' rights for education and verse 2 addresses the government's will to organize nationally integrated education system. Meanwhile, Act 32 highlights the government's attempt to develop Indonesia's national culture along with the citizens' participatory to maintain it. In economy, Act 33 underlines the economy system designed for the citizens leading to the state's ownership for significant economy branches which will be used for the societies' benefits as well as the care for the poors and ignored children under the state's maintenance as written on Act 34. As well, Indonesia guarantees the citizens' right for their state of beliefs and religions according to their options as figured out in Act 29 verse 2.

Indonesia signed up Millennium Development Goals (MDGs) designed by United Nations 2001-2015, in which this program was presented with the goals to eradicate poverty in the state's development strategy. In Indonesia, despite the success to reduce poverty, MDGs is criticized due to its incapacity to figure out the root of poverty, inattentiveness towards inclusiveness, and sustainable development. Furthermore, the absence towards gender equality and human rights is the point of MDGs failure in Indonesia since it recorded high level of gender inequality based on Gender Inequality Index around 0.49-0.60 based on UNDP measurement data in 2011 [1]

As the continuity of MDGs, a model of development strategy which underlines more holistic, humanist, inclusive, and sustainable is established. With the highlight of 17 goals, Sustainable Development Goals visibly has principal purposes to eradicate poverty and hunger as well as to reduce domestic and inter-countries imbalance, to improve water and energy management and to take urgent steps to overcome climate shifts. To present a difference from MDGs, SDGs confirms the urgency addressing the elimination of poverty through joint-efforts strategically. It leads to the economy development, social policies dealing with the fulfillment of various social requirements, such as education, health, and working opportunities along with the ones for resolving climate changes and environment protection. Inclusiveness is the primary point within the SDGs implementation worldwide; therefore, it confirms several goals with a great tendency to eradicate inequality towards vulnerable groups, one of which is LGBTI[2], in this paper transwomen and their gap with the existing circumstances in Indonesia are highlighted due to their issue of formal work attainment. It is undeniable that they have been facing inequality problems addressing the attainment. Particularly in Indonesia where the group is meeting various types of persecutions leading to legal criminalization plan, more complex circumstances will hinder them to struggle for their rights, mainly to attain formal work as part of SDGs goals, such to end poverty in all its form everywhere, to eliminate inequality, and to promote well being for all.

With the ratifications of some covenants regarding human and civil rights to the state laws in Indonesia, the country is supposed to initiate the process of eliminating any discrimination towards minorities, including transwomen, however, it is not a smooth running since most of society layers in Indonesia still are considering their existence immoral, therefore they think of numerous ways to "normalize" them based on their origin of sex when being born instead of respecting their confirmed rights. As a consequence, insurmountable discrimination practices heading to legal criminalization [3]continuously emerge along with the absence of the government attention, including the right fulfillment of transwomen in terms of formal work attainment despite the state's approval to sign SDGs.

---

[1] http://theicph.com/id_ID/id_ID/icph/sustainable-development-goals/ illustrates Indonesia as one of the developing countries with high level of gender inequality level by UNDP analysis

[2] Soliman-Martinez, Madgy, Ending LGBTI Discrimination Is Key To Achieving SDGs, September 29, 2015 highlights how SDGs embody a powerful commitment to achieving a life of dignity for all, including LGBTI people

[3] Dalidjo, Nurdiyansah, Babak Baru Perjuangan LGBT di Indonesia, Category : Gender dan Seksualitas, November 30, 2017,

2. RESEARCH METHODOLOGY

This paper applies a qualitative methodology which relies on gaining the relevant information through two ways; they are interview with significant key person addressing the discussion topic and literature study involving media examination through the cases which discuss most obstacles experienced by transwomen in attaining formal works for their earning.

The interview is conducted based on specific questions in regard to confirming how the keyperson experienced some challenges when attempting to enter the area of formal work and existing strains in the present time for transwomen generally to be working in formal sectors as well as their preference to working in informal ones to earn for living. The experience reveals how the difficulties to enter the formal works begin from the early steps of assessment up to the final interview.

Literature study exposes academic references in accordance with the discussed topic, starting from the basic information about transwomen and human rights based issues, the issues of transwomen to attain formal work, and the state's ratifications of UN covenants to the state's laws referring to human rights issues and SDGs recommendations about inequality eradication. In addition, media examination highlights what cases of transwomen gap to be employed in formal sectors and other general discrimination practices experienced by them as well as what existing solutions have been implemented in purpose to overcome the gap and discrimination issues towards transwomen in Indonesia.

3. DISCUSSION

3.1. The State's Ratification of UN Covenants about Human and Civil Rights to Affirm the Citizens' Rights with No Exceptions

Through the ratification of International Covenant on Civil and Political Rights and Optional Protocol to the International Covenant on Civil and Political Rights to The State Law of Republic of Indonesia No. 12 Year 2005 about The Legalization of International Covenant On Civil And Political Rights along with The Declaration for Act 1[4], Indonesia has credentialed the citizens' civil and political rights as a part of general human rights regardless the positions of sex, ethnicity, race, religion, and sexual orientation. In a broader sense, the state officially provides a legal protection for the citizens towards their rights, such as the rights of life, freedom and personal security, equal treatment on behalf of legal

---

[4] Mengenal Konvenan Internasional Hak Sipil dan Politik, Institute For Criminal Justice Reform, May, 14, 2012 www.icjr.or.id

justice, and personal expressions. All of them are referring to the in line implementation of The Indonesia Constitution 1945 as the citizens' basic rights guaranteed by the state's government. Based on all of them, inexplicitly the state provides the credential for transwomen as a part of Indonesians citizens alongside with their rights, including their chance for better work attainment.

3.2. SDGs' Credentials for the Principle "No one Left Behind" as An Inclusiveness for Transwomen's Right for Work Attainment

According to UNSTATS (UN Statements)[5], discussing SDGs means to embrace everyone's dignity through profound commitments in terms of discontinuance of violence and discrimination practices based on sexual orientations and gender identity covering LGBTI. This statement has been endorsed by 12 UN entities - UNDP, OHCHR, UNAIDS, ILO, UNESCO, UNFPA, UNICEF, UNHCR, UN Women, UNODC, WFP and WHO. Internationally, despite the statement, the UN secretary Ki Moon highlights LGBTI's rights as one of the greatly neglected human rights challenge all the time. It is said due to the contra among the religion conservatives with their penchant to repudiate LGBTI's issues according to existing heteronormative values.

3.3. Transwomen Gap in Indonesia For A Formal Work Attainment as Another Issue for SDGs' Achievement

Transwomen in Indonesia have been existing in Indonesia even before this state was officially established. By tradition and culture[6], for example, Bugis society in South Sulawesi had acknowledged gender variety, particularly before Islam came to the province. In general, they were divided into five parts, oroane (male), makkunrai (female), male similar to female (calabai), female similar to make (calalai), and androgynous priest (bissu). As well, in Toraja society admitted the third gender identity, male similar to female called as burake tambolang. Transgender local belief leaders in Bugis and Toraja were credited with their significant roles in their communities, such as leading spiritual ceremonies or harvesting rituals. Certainly, for the societies it is such a pride when seeing and being invited to above-mentioned ceremonies and rituals. In contrast, the introduction of heteronormative values by colonialists through religion values to the traditional societies

---

[5] Soliman-Martinez, Madgy, Ending LGBTI Discrimination Is Key To Achieving SDGs, September 29, 2015 confirms UNDP to join in the UN statement on ending violence and discrimination based on gender identity and sexual orientation added by involving the endorsement from 12 UN entities

[6] Hidayana, Martua, Irwan, Keberagaman Gender di Indonesia, Sabtu, 15 September 2018, www.kompas.com explores about gender identities variations in Indonesia by tradition and culture, here by taking the example from Bugis society in Sulawesi

eliminated the above-mentioned practices gradually. The values are strictly a part of any "incoming" religions which were brought and introduced to wider groups of societies in Indonesia at that time. Therefore, directly the positions of transgender have no longer become significant and more underestimated due to their status as sinners and religion values violators. Indonesia, as one of the biggest religious countries in the world, obviously respects the heteronormative values while disregarding the existence of other gender identities, and this condition leads to the rising of discriminative and violating practices, including the marginalizing gap for transwomen particularly to attain better chance for formal work.

From the respected to the marginalized, it is the position of transgender, particularly transwomen, in reality not only in Indonesia but also other countries generally. The most visible discrimination occurs when it comes to the issue of their economy right fulfillment.

In Indonesia, based on an observation conducted when having one of gathering activities in S. P.[7](a group of transwomen) Bandung, one of their initiators named R. confirmed that most of the transwomen in the group came from various family backgrounds, from the haves to the poors, and they were in the same issue when being observed from their statements: economy issue. They struggled in such unbelievable ways to survive economically. Most people view them as what they are usually labeled "social disease" and it is because what they always observe on the streets when transwomen work as prostitutes. The label is attached more when they are arrested by the police or other apparatus who often conduct street-raids, such as public order enforcers or publicly acknowledged as satpol PP in the city. They are brought to City's Office of Social enlisting them for a short-time rehabilitation process and are released with their high possibility for them to return to the streets. It occurs simultaneously without integrated program from the office while the label for them is still attached.

R. added that the headquarter of S. P. functioned as a temporary shelter as well as a center of empowerment for transwomen around Bandung. However, she admitted that to attain work was one of the most complicated obstacles since it is very rare to discover transwomen with high levels of education. Some of them used to be in the university for their study, however when graduated, they altered to be transwomen; hence the problem began when thinking of pursuing their careers after university. As a solution, practically they come to gain informal work sectors, such as waitress, masseurs, spa therapists, and hairstylist and make up artists, dancers, and cook in several catering services. Some of them are trapped in the circle of night life working as karaoke guides or strippers in some gay-

---

[7] An interview with R., a founder and initiator of S. P., who emphasizes the movement for empowering transwomen in Bandung. I interviewed her in our School of Peace activity named Craft for Peace in July 2018. She elaborated the general issues faced by transwomen, not only in HIV/AIDS but also in the way of making them empowered economically with their own challenge from their families and surrounding.

suspected night clubs. On the other side, another interview with one young transwoman, A.,[8] revealed about conservatism in formal work sectors which emphasizes the importance of gender identity in working attainment. As a university graduate, she was aware of the complexity for most transwomen to attain formal work in terms of gaining better economy life. She used to face some conditions which almost accepted her to work in some companies, yet the final interviews figured out her status as transwoman and gradually she was uncontacted for signing working contracts. The different condition emerge when applying for entertainment and creative industries, she was well accepted to work in two radio stations despite experiencing some bullying treatments from her partners, and they stopped the bullies after she conducted hormone replacement therapy to be women. Now she is working in Bali as a part of digital marketing team in hope to open properties business there. She highlighted one problem from one of her employer candidates who finally declined her to work in spite of managing to run the final interview. The interviewer said that he actually had no objection to accept her to work, yet the problem relied on her ID card stating her sex was male while in appearance it was she as female. It would confuse all people when having a company visit and having to hand the ID card, then it was about to affect the company's reputation where she planned to work.

Similar situation occurred in India when Hyderabad-based Chandramukhi Muvvala[9], a transwoman was a successful news anchor with a regional Telugu channel. In 2014, she had her own commentary and political analysis show. And then, someone from the senior management thought having a transwoman on air did not make the channel look good. Six months later, Chandramukhi was laid off, although she was never told why in so many words. There was no discrimination from her colleagues though. She added that most interviewers were more interested in her anatomy and sex life than her skills as news anchor. Other issues regarding transwomen employment might occur in terms of their differences from other vulnerable groups, such as women, people of color, race-ethnicity, and disabled due to people's judgment from the sides of immorality and stigma added with some existing problems connecting with identity management, homophobic, and heterosexism.

The above-mentioned illustration provides a huge gap connecting with the plan of SDGs achievement, particularly in Indonesia. As the country which has signed international covenants about civil and human rights, Indonesia is supposed to create humanist environment for their citizens without exceptions addressing their rights, mainly the right for proper living in economy terms and one of this means open working opportunity for

---

[8] I met A. in our School of Peace class meeting discussing about gender and sexuality. We discussed about her issue to gain a formal work attainment up to her personal decision why becoming transwomen was the one she wanted for her life. It was conducted in August, 2018

[9] Mantri, Geetika, Workplace Horrors: Why Formal Employment Is A Distant Dream For The Transgender Community, An Article, December 17, 2016

any citizen regardless their backgrounds of gender identities. As mentioned before that SDGs reflects a principle of "no one left behind" , therefore all countries signing this are expected to embrace LGBTI, in this paper it highlights transwomen who struggle for their right to attain work opportunity in formal sectors as well as embraces them to be a part of the state's development actors.

3. CONCLUSION AND RECOMMENDATION

Some failures in Indonesia MDGs implementation referring to gender issues which underline the slow conduction of gender equality become a comprehensive reflection before the undergoing of SDGs. The state must be in high capacity to respond this since in fact they provide a number of relevant state' laws along with their derivative regulations in each province and lower level regions, therefore their existence should be able to empower the people with the issues as prioritized. The state laws in accordance with SDGs goals are expected to cover all citizens 'rights with no exceptions as the point of SDGs cites the principle of "no one left behind". One of the targets of SDGs is to involve vulnerable groups in a large scale and it should be performed by providing broad opportunity for transwomen, as one of vulnerable groups in Indonesia. The opportunity which should be provided while challenging for the government and society is to present formal works attainment for them, in which this will obviously come up with protests due to most society' unacceptance for the group after being indicated as disrespectful to existing religion and social values in Indonesia. Furthermore, the situation causes most of them discredited with low economy living added with uncertain income from informal working sectors while at the same time they are stigmatized as a part of social disease, required to be rehabilitated to be as the sex they are born instead of respecting their rights as human as mentioned in various covenants and state's laws after the ratification.

SDGs' accomplishment in Indonesia is still in the progress through some state's laws addressing the issues of development and it is certain that the government in general is supposed to guard the overall implementations. Particularly about the working attainment in formal sectors for transwomen, the government should wisely open their mind about their existence and consider some significant ways to cover their rights in terms of their economy right fulfillment. This process requires gradual process, starting from perspective introduction about vulnerable groups, one of which is transwomen, to the government officials and apparatuses since they are the keys for public policies. In the following time, the introduction of SDGs platforms and goals is supposed to be acknowledged by public in acceptable terms and language while emphasizing to the human rights respect priority as a way leading to the development based on the principle of balance for anyone. Next is the making and socialization of affirmative policies regarding the state's credentials towards vulnerable groups, here is transwomen, to access their rights with no discriminations according to SDGs goals. In gradual periods, for example, in USA[10], in 2001 almost 900 companies enacted non discrimination policies covering sexual orientations including 10 states and 106 local government agencies workers who were protected in their work stations on the basis of sexual orientations.

The following question will quite remain in our mind: will the Indonesian government have a strong willingness to be attentive towards transwomen's existence and their rights?

---

[10] M. Hash, Kristina and Ceperish, D. Sherry, Workplaces Issues, page 408, from Sexual Orientation and Gender Expression in Social Work Practice (Working with Gay, Lesbian, Bisexual, and Transgender People) Edited by Morrow, F. Deana and Messinger, Lori, 2006, Columbia University Press, New York.

REFERENCES

1. M. Hash, Kristina and Ceperish, D. Sherry, Workplaces Issues, page 408, from Sexual Orientation and Gender Expression in Social Work Practice (Working with Gay, Lesbian, Bisexual, and Transgender People) Edited by Morrow, F. Deana and Messinger, Lori, 2006, Columbia University Press, New York.

2. Langlois J, Anthony, Human Rights, Part IV The New Agenda : Globalization and Global Governance, Associate Professor of International Relations in The School of International Studies, Flinders University, 2017, Cambridge University Press.

3. Muhr Louise, Sara, Sullivan Rose, Katie, and Rich, Craig. Situated Transgressiveness: Exploring One's Transwomen's Lived Experiences Across Three Situation Contexts, May 26, 2015.

4. Wilkinson, Cai and Langlois J, Anthony, Special Issue: Not Such an International Human Right Norm? Local Resistance to Lesbian, Gay, Bisexual, and Transgender Rights-Preliminary Comments from Journal of Human Rights, 2014, Taylor and Francis Groups.

5. Basil, Alexander, Confessing Society, Confessing Cis-Tem Rethinking Consent Through Images of Transpeople in Media Frontiers : a Journal of Women Studies, Vol 39 no 2, June 2, 2018.

6. Kit, Dorey, The Sustainable Development Goals and LGBT Inclusion, London: Stonewall International, 2016

7. The Sustainable Development Goals Report 2016, www.unstats.un.org/sdgs/report/2016/leaving-no-one-behind

8. Soliman-Martinez, Madgy, Ending LGBTI Discrimination Is Key To Achieving SDGs, September 29, 2015
www.undp.org/content/undp/en/home/blog/2015/9/29/Ending-discrimination-based-on-gender-identity-and-sexual-orientation-is-key-to-achieving-the-SDGs.html

9. Mengenal Konvenan Internasional Hak Sipil dan Politik, Institute For Criminal Justice Reform, May, 14, 2012 www.icjr.or.id

10. Dalidjo, Nurdiyansah, Babak Baru Perjuangan LGBT di Indonesia, Category : Gender dan Seksualitas, November 30, 2017,
www.magdalene.co/news/-1519-babak-baru-perjuangan-lgbt-di-Indonesia.html

11. Mantri, Geetika, Workplace Horrors: Why Formal Employment Is A Distant Dream For The Transgender Community, An Article, December 17, 2016
www.thenewsminute.com/article/workplace-horrors-why-formal-employment-distant-dream-transgender-community-54418

12. Hidayana, Martua, Irwan, Keberagaman Gender di Indonesia, Sabtu, 15 September 2018, www.kompas.com